The University of Toledo Press
Copyright © 2014
All rights reserved
Manufactured in the United States of America
*Can I Get A Witness*
By John Gibbs Rockwood
ISBN: 978-0-932259-41-7
Editor, Joel Lipman
Book design by Andrew Grady
Project assistance by Zach Fischel and Jasmine Townsend
Cover photograph by John Gibbs Rockwood
www.utoledopress.com

# Can I Get

# A Witness

## John Gibbs Rockwood

# Table of Contents

**Intro** — **001**

**1970s** — **006**

**1980s** — **064**

**1990s** — **122**

## 2000s 150

## About John Gibbs Rockwood 158

## Acknowledgments 160

## Index 162

## First and Foremost
John Gibbs Rockwood

First and foremost, my heartfelt thanks and love to my sweet wife, Jennifer, who is so patient with my late nights, photo frenzies, and chaotic blues lifestyle. She held my vision with faith in me all along. Gratitude to my sons, Ian and Julian, for all the aspects of life and music they've taught me and for their reverence for the camera. Thanks to Molly and Ashley, my sons' amazing spouses, who enrich all our lives, and to Everett, who came into the world last year, ready to sing with his grandpa. Love and respect to the Rockwood clan—Kathy, Nancy, Mary, Sarah, Timmy, and Jeff—who helped me make my way.

I'm indebted to my *Can I Get A Witness* team who helped me get this up and out—Joel Lipman, John Adams, Tom Barden, Molly Schiever, and Drew Grady, and to Dorothy Siegel, Angie Cherry Jones, Bob Seeman, Steve Hansen, Mel Dusseau, Barbara Floyd, Jasmine Townsend, and the production and design staff of the University of Toledo Press.

I recognize those greats in my life who are gone now—Big Jack Reynolds, S.P. Leary, Detroit Junior, Ron Crawdaddy Crawford, Roosevelt Hatcher, Bill French, Eddie Kirkland, Art Griswold, Dave Ray, Glenn Osborn, Piano Fats, Howard Armstrong, The Coachman, Henry Griffin, Roman Griswold, and Robert Jr. Lockwood.

I thank the big movers, shakers and dear friends who've come and gone along the way: Sir Mack Rice, Bill and Ruth Cone, Jim O'Neal, Greg Oatis, Walter Salwitz, Johnny Newmark, Bob Seger, Pat O'Connor, John Sinclair, David Yonke, Phil Hazard, Russ Kadri, Mike Sallah, Ximena Gray, Joe Buehler, Rod Lockwood, Leni Sinclair, Michael Robert Frank, R.J. Spangler, Jim Kenzie, Dave Athanas, Steve Athanas, Brett Bonner, Robert Whitehall Jr., Robert Gordon, Geary Chansley, Harmonica Shah, B.B. King, Ian McLagen, Clifford Murphy, John Nicholas, Dave Gierke, Sue Riser, Nick Stevens, Nick Muska, and Mike Miller.

And a nod to the contributing cool people, music, places, and good reads I've encountered: Voodoo Libido, Queens of Harmony, The Dynatones, Blue-Suit Records, Delmark Records, Chess Records, Earwig Music, Culture Clash Records, Boogie Records, University of Mississippi Blues Archives, Black Swamp Arts Festival, *Living Blues Magazine,* Madhouse Gallery, Backstage Gallery, *The Toledo Blade, Toledo Free Press, Toledo City Paper,* Hines Farm, the Ottawa Tavern, *Big City Blues Magazine*, the Haircuts, Graceland, Mississippi Blues Trail, Boogie Woogie Red, Bill Schurk, Pat Adams, Arhoolie Records, Toledo Museum of Art, and the Sunday Night Root Hoot.

To all those named and to all those unfairly forgotten,
thanks for being with me on this big blue ball.

## Foreground to the background: Observing John Rockwood
Walter Salwitz, The Dynatones

There in the parking lot lay the decomposing body. It was a '53 DeSoto leaning on broken springs and in the last shudders of its death throes. In the back seat was a huge black man playing a guitar.

"Man, I think that's Big Joe Williams." Rockwood's circling the beat-up car and its occupants like downed prey. He's snapping pics fast, being very careful, shadowy, cautious, alert.

Turns out it was Big Joe. He and Bukka White drove up from Cottonsack, Mississippi, to deliver Son House to the Ann Arbor Blues Fest. The year was '68 or '69, a mythical moment, and someone had given Rockwood a Nikon camera.

That camera would change John Rockwood's life forever. Growing up in Toledo, Ohio, you learned to take advantage of any outside stimuli that came your way, and John did. He was already playing harmonica in local bands, and he was painting, mushing around with acrylics, achieving a sort of a Broderick Crawford meets Picasso effect.

"Hey, Walt. Ike and Tina Turner are at the Black Horse in Covington, Kentucky, this weekend." Now, how in the hell did he know that? We are not talking internet around 1970, more like talking drums or having your ear on the rail.

"Bobo Jenkins is playing on Plum Street in Detroit next Monday." Just where or how Rockwood got his info I don't know, perhaps channeling Robert Johnson. He had to know what was going on and let everybody else in on it. Out there in the dark Midwest night he just knew who was playing.

Now here's the scoop—he was spreading the word. Consumed with the fire, he was selling us tickets to his personal revival of the music.

John's unique timing in shutter exposure puts him in rarefied territory. He's a performer on both sides of the camera, knowing just when to blow, when to lay out. No poses, just sneaking around getting the true sweat and funk of the moment, like Rocky Colavito poised and relaxed, waiting on an inside curve, waiting for the sweet spot. Then the trigger.

John's introduced us to a nearly uncountable number of rock 'n' roll, blues, and jazz musicians, sometimes performing with them, sometimes accompanying them on his camera like it's a musical instrument. He works in black and white, the way Monet worked in pastels. Always keeping it real, straight up, black and white.

It's been a long show and we should all be very pleased to have a cat like John Gibbs Rockwood around to show us what we missed.

—Everglades City, Florida

# IN CONCERT
John Gibbs Rockwood

## Being up close

The reason I got up close was because I got a camera. And the reason I got a camera was, of course, so I could get up close. That's where it all came together. I was never afraid of getting right in the face of the performers, leaning down at their feet to feel the shot. I wanted the lines, the wigs and brims, the tear ducts, the sand, the life story in their faces, the pissed-offness in the eyes because the guarantee didn't come through or somebody drank all the beer in the dressing room.

And I got to meet my heroes, be there with a camera when, at the end of the night, there was no money to pay the musicians, the crowd was gone, and so were the promoters. I was there witnessing the astounding games and rip-offs these great musicians put up with. I was there one night across the Ambassador Bridge in Windsor [Ontario] when James Brown went on when he knew he wasn't going to get paid—he totally knocked 'em out, dressed in a kilt.

That camera took me to places like Clarksdale, Mississippi; West Helena, Arkansas; Theresa's in Chicago; South Halsted Street, funky basement dressing rooms, smoky plywood hockey arena floors with amps stacked for a wall of sound that blew back your hair, crowds big and small waiting for airplanes to arrive or busses to depart. That camera caught long gone places in my Toledo hometown—the Sports Arena, Rusty's, Elvis in a white suit at the University of Toledo Centennial Hall, the Dynatones and Big Jack Reynolds at the Ottawa Tavern, Rock, Rhythm & Blues festivals in Promenade Park.

I became a driver, a roadie, an adult, a messenger, and a confidant. I drove for Chinese take-out in Detroit and falafel and hummus in Toledo. I reached under the front seat for half-pints of whiskey. And, once a level of trust was established, I was a friend. I met John Sinclair the day he got out of prison. I knocked hard three times on the door of Otis Ruslt's trailer because regardless of the wreckage of life, the show must go on, whether it's Tiny Tim in his Pampers, Nashville or Memphis, a cradle of music or a dive in the boonies, the studios of Chess Records, Fortune Records, Sun Records.

So I was right there with the lens and shutter. It didn't matter whether I knew an F-stop from a stop sign, a light meter from a parking meter, I was snapping—tap dancers, comediennes, side men, shills and hangers on, two-or three-day job singers, jokesters, and the best damn musicians playing rock 'n' roll and blues low and high at hippie festivals, in rough halls, theaters, and sleazy venues. Right there, up close.

## During the performance

Even before the lights go down at a rock concert, you know the first couple of songs are going to be kick-ass, whether it's the Rolling Stones Tour of the Americas for two-and-a-half hours in Cleveland Municipal Stadium in 1975, or Art Griswold soloing outside Theo's

Taverna on Summit Street in Toledo, or Jack Owens from Mississippi with his five gold teeth and sidekick Bud Spires on a hand harp, the Mississippi saxophone.

Performing is about spotlights and straw hats, James Brown wearing a dress, H. Bomb Ferguson raising a bony finger, Muddy Waters commanding the stage like a Buddha, Jerry Lee Lewis arriving one-and-a-half hours late with two bimbos falling out of the limousine, taking the stage like a murderer on the run, and opening up with Hank Williams' "You Win Again." You forget about The Clash, the Sex Pistols, and Johnny Rotten, all the tattoo bad boys of rock 'n' roll, 'cause he's The Killer and no one gets out of the house alive after Jerry Lee Lewis plays.

Performance might be the sound of Boston Blackie over a fuzzed out, fractured sound system on the South Side of Chicago, Little Wolf in a wrinkled fifty-year-old tuxedo, performing late at night for white guys from Toledo, Ohio, rumored to be big-time record producers. Sometimes performance anticipates the show, like the time before a concert when Paul Stanley of KISS said, "I want to tell you something—I don't want you to raise your head for the first two songs, cause if you do it's gonna get blown off when the flames and fire come up." I kept my head down and got the shot.

Sometimes it's too bright. Sometimes the roll comes out blank. Sometimes it comes out dark. Then there's the good ones.

Ultimately there are two kinds of shots between the wall and the stage at a rock show, where you're waiting for the crowd to press forward and the bouncers to flee. You crawl under the stage, under the steel support cables and reward yourself with a trip to the dressing room for a Heineken and a champagne glass of booze.

And not to forget that there's the festival shot and there's the danger shot, especially when you're in Clarksdale and you invade someone's privacy. Either way, you don't check nothing, you just shoot.

And then there's the shot you didn't take, the one that's in your head forever.

## The Backstage Pass

Backstage is the place everybody wants to be. It's a sanctum. It could be a john … guitars laid out by roadies across urinals for Mick Ralphs to check before going on stage.

Sometimes the backstage isn't all it's cracked up to be—it can be groupies, sycophants, overzealous security guards—but there's power in that laminate card, that laminate that says "I'm with the band." He's with the band, he's OK.

Some of the guys are very warm. Some of the girls are very warm, too. And you travel, to Clarksdale, to Memphis, you go to Chicago—that laminate will get you anywhere. You slide in the limo with Richie Blackmore of Deep Purple, who says, "You ride in the back seat." It's like you're the rock star, you've got the laminate.

At the end of the show, you jump back into the limo and there's a floor in the hotel with four rooms blacked out. Up you go with the roadies, the groupies, the instruments. Who knows what's next?

It doesn't matter whether it's Theresa's or the Checkerboard Lounge, here or there, they come up close to you or maybe say from a distance, "It's gonna close," and then it's so long—to Gene Simmons of KISS, goodbye to Phil Guy or Dave Alvin of The Blasters, and you remember times when Koko Taylor was alive or Freddie King was alive or Albert King was alive or Big Jack was sitting in a metal folding chair. Each time you say goodbye it could be for the last time or the next time.

You're on a tour bus with Freddie King when he's making out with his girlfriend. You're talking to Albert King's son in the dressing room and you say, "Who drives the big van out there?" and he says "Albert does. Albert does all the driving."

I've been to places where there's nothing more than a light bulb over the stage. We pull up and there's only two cars, so we go to town to get a burger and come back and Junior Kimbrough's playing and R.L. Burnside's playing and the cornfield's full of cars and everything is getting disoriented. The ladies are dressed up in tight jeans and booties, doing the snake hip dance. Then, later, it's four o'clock in the morning and there's gunshots and the man says, "Don't worry. It's just gunplay and we've still got beer."

And you realize instantly you've been to a place where few people have been and where many people have gone.

**Waylon Jennings, 1970s**
Sports Arena
Toledo, Ohio

The great Waylon Jennings looking down from the stage. He turned that hockey hall into a rockin' honky tonk cafe.

**Jerry Shirley, 1970s**
Sports Arena
Toledo, Ohio

The drummer from Humble Pie backstage at the Sports Arena. After he left Natural Gas he went on to be a big time disk jockey in Cleveland. Now he's back in England.

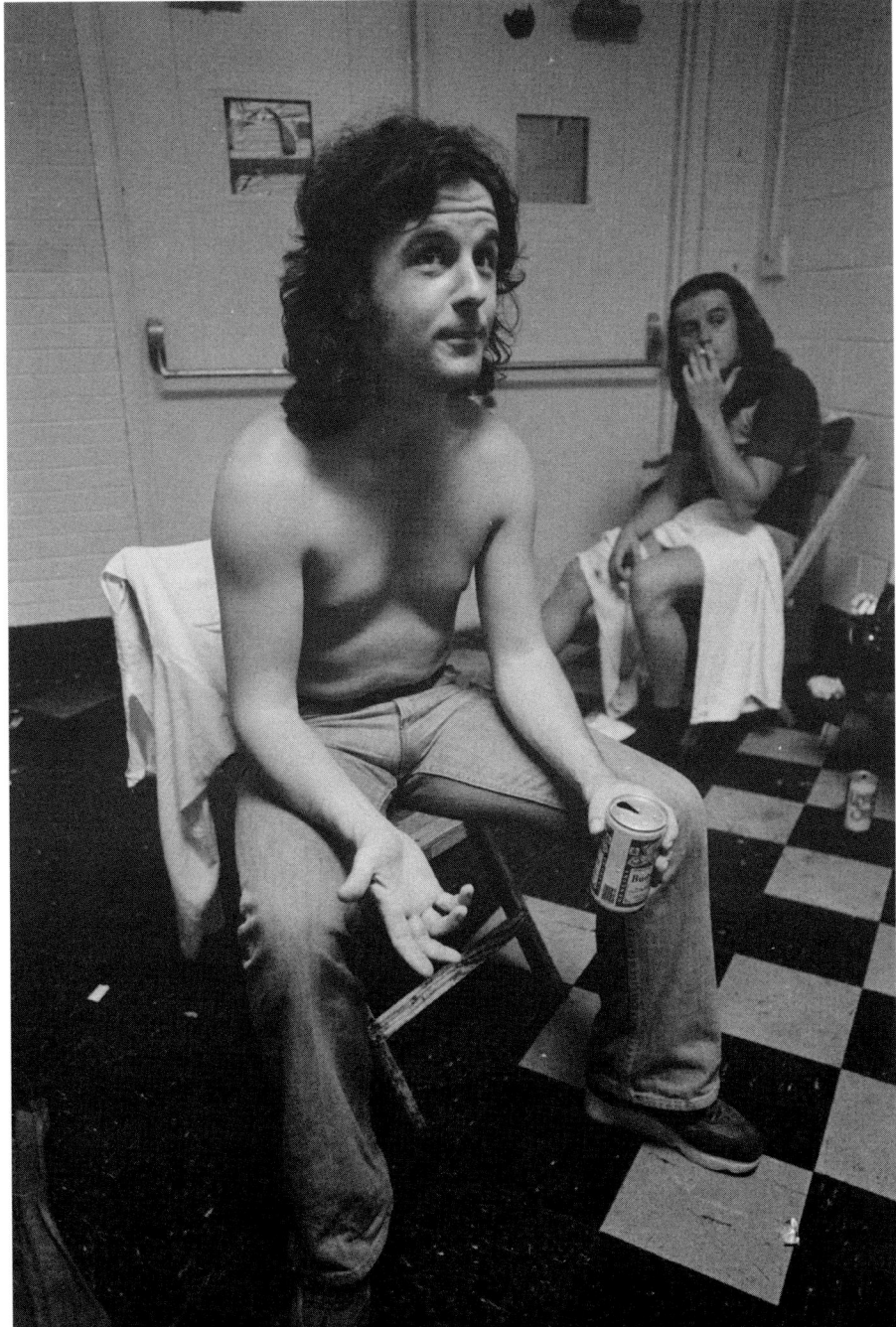

**Gregg Allman, 1970s**
O'Hara Arena,
Dayton, Ohio

We'd travel all over to shows. This is after Duane [Allman] died and we went down to Dayton to see the Allman Brothers at this big arena. You can see by the crowd Gregg had everybody stunned. Bud on the keyboards, smoke in the air, a gone time.

**Houston Stackhouse, 1974**
Ann Arbor Blues Festival,
Ann Arbor, Michigan

Houston was a member of Sonny Boy Williamson II's band in West Helena, Arkansas. He sang a great cover of Tommy Johnson's "Canned Heat."

**Mick Ralphs, Bad Company, 1970s**
Sports Arena
Toledo, Ohio

In the famous Green Room, or the men's latrine, at the Toledo Sports Arena, Mick Ralphs of Bad Company checking out the guitars with the band's roadies.

**Ritchie Blakemore, 1970s**
Olympia Stadium
Detroit, Michigan

I always dug that shadow, the stage show of heavy rock 'n' roll.

**Glenn Cornick, 1970s**
Sports Arena
Toledo, Ohio

Glenn Cornick backstage before the Sports Arena show. He was also in Paris, a '70s power trio that didn't last too long. He always wore this crazy outfit.

**Roosevelt Sykes, 1970s**
Blind Pig
Ann Arbor, Michigan

New Orleans piano master Roosevelt Sykes and I set up this photo. I took him into a closet in the basement of the Blind Pig and had a guy hold a lamp next to his head, then we shot the picture. They called him "Honey Dripper" cuz' he was so sweet to the ladies.

**Paul Stanley, 1970s**
Sports Arena
Toledo, Ohio

Paul Stanley puckers up and holds a pose for my camera.

**Stan Mixon, 1970s**
Ann Arbor Blues Fest
Ann Arbor, Michigan

Stan Mixon, bass player for the Joanna Connor Band, says good morning.

**Jerry Reed, 1970s**
In his studio
Toledo, Ohio

The late great Show Dancer Jerry Reed shakes his legs— again. He was famous as a dancer in the '30s and '40s— really a lost art, the vaudeville dancers. Reed invited me up to see him work out in his studio, in a block of Toledo where the Huntington Arena is today.

**Willie Dixon, 1970s**
Mariposa Folk Festival
Toronto, Ontario

What a giant. Wrote for Bo Diddley, the Wolf, Muddy, Otis Rush, wrote "Diddy Wah Diddy," "I'm Ready," "Backdoor Man, "Little Red Rooster," the great "Hootchie Cootchie Man." I was just getting into it back then and Willie Dixon, behind his big upright bass, invited me backstage. There was free beer, BBQ, and there was Bobby Blue Bland and Buddy Guy. The backstage pass was a sheriff's badge.

**Mac Thompson, 1970**
Ann Arbor Blues Festival
Ann Arbor, Michigan

Chicago bass player
Mac Thompson takes
a break in Windsor.

**John Sinclair, 1971**
Detroit, Michigan

John Sinclair, Flint native, manager of the MC5, musician, D.J., blues historian. You know, John Lennon did an Ann Arbor concert to get him out after Sinclair was busted and sentenced to twenty years after being set up for two joints. He was released after about six months. This is about a week after the concert and we had an interview up in Detroit.

**Johnny Ace and John Lee Hooker, 1972**
Ann Arbor Blues Festival
Ann Arbor, Michigan

John Lee doesn't play four bar or five bar, he just plays what he wants to play. And he'll start and stop, making guitar changes whenever he wants to. Just look at Ace and you see. "I never took my eyes off the man."

**Freddie King, 1972**
Ann Arbor Blues Festival
Ann Arbor, Michigan

The Texas Cannonball on the guitar.

**Jimmy Reed, 1973**
Ann Arbor Blues Festival
Ann Arbor, Michigan

Wigged up at the Ann Arbor Blues Festival, Reed played a sweet harp and wrote great lyrics, all of 'em really the same shuffly song bent and redone. Listening to his records sometimes you hear his wife whispering the words to him 'cuz he couldn't memorize anything. An original.

**Victoria Spivey and the Brooklyn Blues Busters, 1973**
Ann Arbor Blues Festival
Ann Arbor, Michigan

I love her look, rolling her eyes at bassist Johnny Ace's fro halo.

**Howlin' Wolf, 1973**
Bowen Field House
Eastern Michigan University
Ypsilanti, Michigan

The mighty Howlin' Wolf, one of the heaviest guys I ever saw. When I got there, he was sitting on a basketball riser with his buddies and I walked up to him and said, "Hey, Mr. Burnett, Mr. Wolf, can I get your autograph?" And he goes, "I signed my life away, signing all the wrong stuff. Leave me alone." I was crushed and walking away and I hear this: "Hey boy, don't you want my autograph?" The only thing I had was an old girlfriend's picture. I still have it, signed by Howlin' Wolf on the back. The greatest live performer ever.

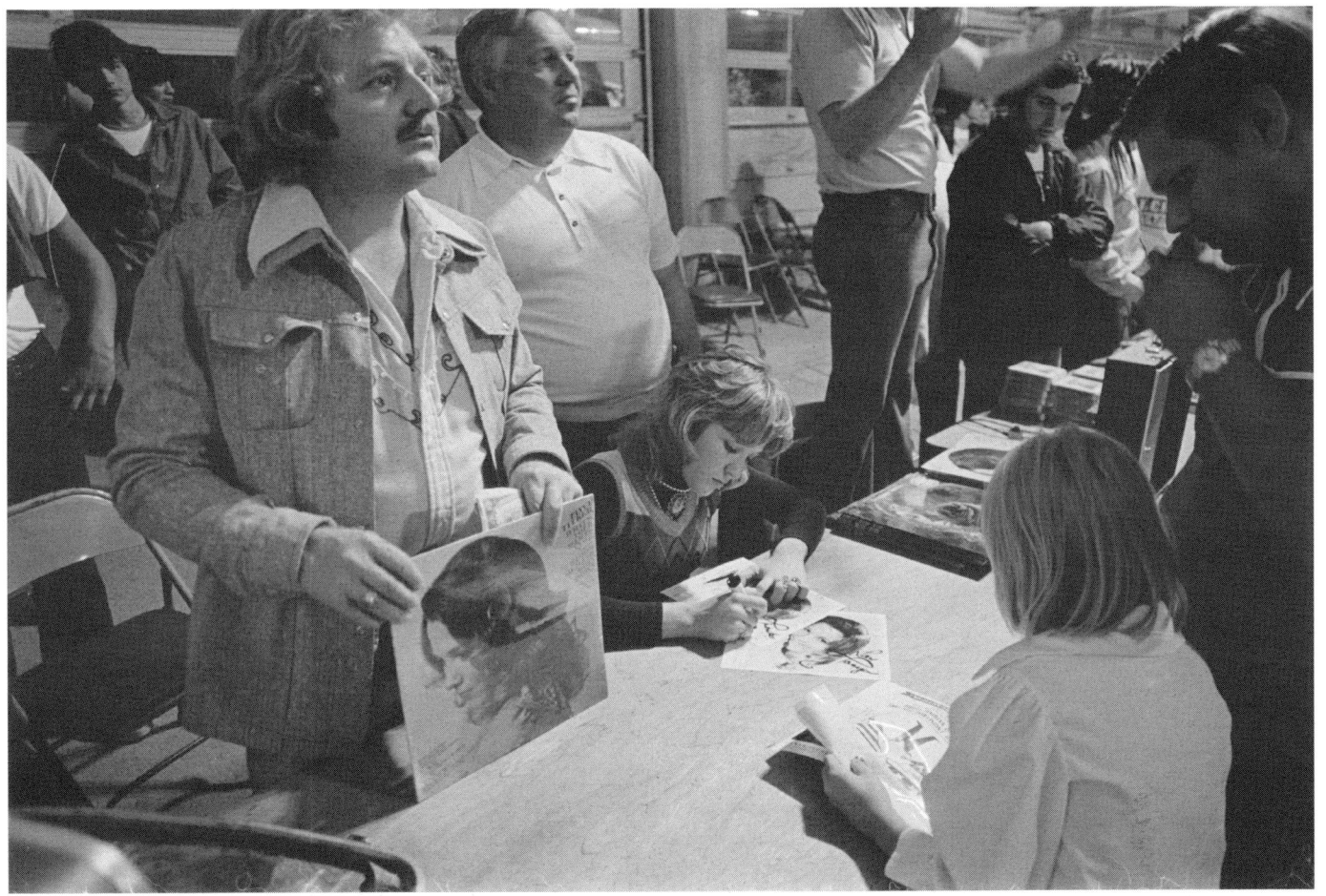

**Tanya Tucker, 1974**
Lucas County Fairgrounds
Toledo, Ohio

Young Tanya Tucker, just sixteen at this point, signing photos and albums after her show at the old Mud Hens Stadium at the Fairgrounds. She performed during the day and this was the first photo assignment I had for a magazine. I was looking for blues but they gave me Tanya. She'd seen her first rock concert the night before, the Allman Brothers. I think that's her pops behind her.

**Son House, 1974**
Mariposa Folk Festival
Toronto, Ontario

You know, man, this great bluesman and artist died and lies in Detroit's blues heaven, Mt. Hazel Cemetery. The Detroit Blues Society held a benefit concert to raise money for a marker. Mariposa was one of his last performances.

**Leslie West, 1974**
Sports Arena
Toledo, Ohio

Mountain's big hit at the time was "Mississippi Queen." Even though he lost a leg a couple of years ago, Leslie West is still playing. This shot's just before he took the stage at the Sports Arena.

**Muddy Waters, 1974**
Sports Arena
Toledo, Ohio

Muddy Waters holding court for a bunch of his fans backstage. Now that was just a party.

**John Lee Hooker with Bobo Jenkins, 1974**
Ann Arbor Blues Festival
Ann Arbor, Michigan

The great boogie bopper, John Lee Hooker, sharing a laugh with Bobo Jenkins and some of his old pals from Detroit. The guy stuttered a lot, which you can't tell on his records. One of my heroes.

**James Brown, 1974**
Windsor, Ontario

In his outfit and dressed to kill, James Brown knew he wasn't going to get paid, 'cause by Sunday the money was gone. My buddy said let's go up front and get by the stage and take some pictures. So I'm sitting there, man, and taking pictures, but water keeps getting on the lens. I'm thinking like, "Ah it's raining." Well, it was James Brown's sweat.

**David Bowie, 1974**
Young Americans Tour
Detroit, Michigan

He had a full soul band with him at a theater up in Detroit that I can't recall the name of. Anyhow, a theater in Detroit. And to get these shots I had to sneak my camera into the theater all broken down in parts, lenses in socks, film in my underwear, camera hanging around the back of my neck.

**Peter Frampton, 1974**
Agora Ballroom
Toledo, Ohio

He'd just left Humble Pie and was on the road to super stardom… young Peter Frampton at the Agora, which is gone now, along with Frampton's hair. A hell of a guy.

**One String Sam, 1974**
Sports Arena
Toledo, Ohio

One String Sam played a one-string guitar. He'd zip a single string and sing into an empty baby food jar. He cut one single and made 300 dollars and his one song was "I Need 300 Dollars To Get My Baby Out Of Jail." It was true; he took his money and got his lady out. Sam tore it up, was an amazing guy. He was also a magic guy. He'd run around with Muddy Waters and those guys, twist his ear, and silver dollars would fall out of his nose. Here he's in his Sports Arena dressing room.

**Daryl Hall and John Oates, 1974**
Field House
University of Toledo
Toledo, Ohio

Philly Soul greats Hall and Oates, in the dressing room of the old UT Field House, a photo that actually wound up included in their 2009 box set.

**Frank Zappa, 1974**
Sports Arena
Toledo, Ohio

Listening to questions, Frank Zappa holds court backstage at the Sports Arena. One of the straightest, stone cold sober, most intellectual guys I ever met. No drugs, no booze, no nothin'. He had a thermos of coffee and the *Wall Street Journal* on his desk.

**JB Hutto, 1974**
Toledo Blues Festival
Toledo, Ohio

In his turban at the '74 Fest, and as was his way, he said almost nothing, but his brutally true slide guitar, just a crushing bottleneck and a voice raw enough to peel chrome off a microphone, rendered additional communication superfluous.

**Lou Reed, 1974**
Field House
University of Toledo
Toledo, Ohio

It was Homecoming and Halloween night in the old UT Field House and there was Lou Reed. A wild, date night concert, Reed was opening for Hall and Oates. So he comes out and takes the mic cord off the stand, ties it around his arm and acts like he's shooting up. He had people freaking out.

**Rolling Stones, 1975**
Cleveland Stadium
Cleveland, Ohio

They're singing "You've Got To Move." The concert was like the World Series of Rock and Roll—you had Billy Preston, J. Geils, Kansas, and tons others. It went on and on and when The Stones finally took the stage, people were throwing M-80s and going crazy, but anyhow it turned out pretty good. We wore casual clothes, sharp suitcoats and ties, and had suitcases full of beer and stuff when we checked in at the hotel 'cause the hotel was freaking out. It was the Holiday Inn and that's gone, too. The next morning we got up and were walking down the hall, and it's just soaked. People got up in the middle of the night, turned on fire hoses, and just destroyed the place.

**Mick Jagger, 1975**
Cleveland Stadium
Cleveland, Ohio

Mick, soaked in sweat, doing his thing at the Mistake on the Lake during the 1975 World Series of Rock. Annual rock concerts were promoted by Belkin Productions at the old Cleveland Stadium during the '70s and there'd be 80,000 hard partying fans going nuts.

**Paul Rodgers of Bad Company, 1975**
Sports Arena
Toledo, Ohio

I spent the day with him. We met up on the tarmac at Toledo Airport when his plane landed. He was all messed up, but it was a kick-ass concert.

**Bonnie Raitt and Sippie Wallace, 1975**
Hill Auditorium
Ann Arbor, Michigan

Sippie Wallace was one of Raitt's big inspirations. They first performed together at the '72 Ann Arbor festival. At the Hill concert, Bonnie brought Wallace up to sing with her on Sippie's song "Women Be Wise." What a great look of affection and respect. Sippie's great granddaughter's the girl behind her.

**Ritchie Havens, 1975**
Poe Ditch Festival
Bowling Green, Ohio

Hard to believe that this is the crowd for a pop music festival at the Bowling Green State University football stadium. They never get near that many for a ball game.

**Joan Baez, 1975**
Toledo Zoo Amphitheater
Toledo, Ohio

I spent the day with her. The band had Jim Gordon and James Jamerson, the astounding session bass player from Motown. Around four o'clock, James came over to me and asked, "Where can I get some wine?" I told him, "Man, it's Sunday. In Ohio you can't get anything." Tickets were about five bucks, with first come seating.

**Atlanta Rhythm Section, 1970s**
Downtown Toledo
Toledo, Ohio

Here's the Atlanta Rhythm Section's drummer, Robert Nix, in downtown Toledo, pointing at Ronnie Hammond, who passed away in 2011. We did an interview and they were playing that night at the Sports Arena, and I had to go up the road to Ypsilanti to do another one with Muddy Waters.

**B.B. King, 1970s**
Sports Arena
Toledo, Ohio

B.B. King is just the ultimate to me. Always very appreciative of his audience … two or three times you'd go back and get in line and one-by-one he'd take you into his little dressing room and sit there and pose for pictures with you or sign albums if you brought them. If you didn't, he had photos he'd sign and give you one. The master, screaming the blues.

**Jethro Tull, 1976**
Sports Arena
Toledo, Ohio

This is Ian Anderson of Jethro Tull eye-balling the big-wigged backup singers. The thing I like about this photo is the way he's looking at that singer like, "Later tonight, baby." Jethro Tull was great when they played the Arena. There were so many bands back then.

**Johnny Shines, 1976**
Jazz Heritage Festival
New Orleans

Backstage, Johnny Shines down in New Orleans at the '76 Jazz Heritage Festival. He'd just got done playing and is having a Dixie Beer in one of those heavy tin cans Dixie used. Shines was Robert Johnson's contemporary. They used to travel together. He went up to Chicago, worked construction, and got back into the music thing, recording for Testament when Chicago electric blues started getting popular.

**Cesar Zuiderwijk, 1976**
Poe Ditch Festival
Bowling Green, Ohio

Cesar was the drummer for the great Dutch band Golden Earring. He's just standing in the trailer door in the sun, looking good, and checking out the festival scene.

**Robbie "Driver of Stars," 1976**
Poe Ditch Festival
Bowling Green, Ohio

This is Rob, Robbie, the driver of stars. He drove all the rock 'n' roll guys. This is backstage in Bowling Green. Ever the gentleman with an eye for attractive women, he's lighting a cig for Colleen.

**Bernie Leadon and Glenn Frey, The Eagles, 1976**
Cincinnati Pop Festival
Cincinnati, Ohio

At the Cincinnati Pop Festival, the Eagles' Bernie Leadon and Glenn Frey tuning up in the back of a semi.

**Nitty Gritty Dirt Band, 1976**
Poe Ditch Festival
Bowling Green, Ohio

Just sitting out front waiting for their show to start, members of the Nitty Gritty Dirt Band warming up in the sun.

**Southside Johnny and the Asbury Jukes, 1970s**
Field House
University of Toledo
Toledo, Ohio

Another one at the UT Field House, right after Bruce Springsteen got huge and Jersey music was in and Southside got popular. He'd signed with Columbia Records. They had a horn section there, powering out. A really great show, and it was my first date with my future wife.

**Elvis Presley, 1977**
Centennial Hall
University of Toledo
Toledo, Ohio

The King's last tour … he was 42. I actually didn't have tickets. A friend was selling his for 75 bucks and I told him, "Sorry, I don't have a dime." Well, he calls me two hours later and says, "You know, I was thinking who should be there. John Rockwood, I'm gonna' give you the tickets." We were in, like, the fourth row.

**Bob Seger and the Silver Bullet Band, 1978**
Sports Arena
Toledo, Ohio

Detroit rocker Bob Seger in concert at the Sports Arena. On his last tour, this vintage Seger photo of mine was used on a T-shirt.

**Paul Stanley and Gene Simmons with Chris Loop, 1979**
Sports Arena
Toledo, Ohio

The KISS guys razzing and posing with Toledo D.J. Chris Loop. They'd taken comic books, rock 'n' roll, kabuki theater, and mixed 'em all together. They were definitely into making money.

**3D, 1979**
Cobo Arena
Detroit, Michigan

3D is a band of my friends that toured with J. Geils. This is Cobo Arena and they're doing a sound check. I love the battered skins.

**Paul Kantner**
**Jefferson Starship, 1979**
Anderson Arena
Bowling Green State University
Bowling Green, Ohio

Kantner writing music and charts in a motel room at that university down the road.

**Findlay Pop Festival, 1970s**
Findlay, Ohio

Lots of coolers and sun and no chairs at the Findlay Pop Festival. Feuding flags could have launched a battle, but music was the common bond.

**KISS, 1980s**
Sports Arena
Toledo, Ohio

I'd spent the day with KISS. They kept saying "Don't take any pictures. You'll get what you want before the show. We'll take care of you." So I'm standing there and they all come out in their makeup. This is Gene Simmons and one of the roadies, obviously having a good time. I mean, this is the Toledo Sports Arena. Paul Stanley took me out front before the show started and he gestured keep your head down during the first two songs; otherwise it's gonna get blown off. Then there's all these smoke bombs, pyrotechnics. KISS comes out and bam bam bam bam bam!

**J. Geils Band, 1980s**
**Sports Arena**
Toledo, Ohio

My friends in 3D opened for J. Geils all around the country when "Love Stinks" came out. The band's playing it and we're looking and looking and here comes Peter Wolf floating down from the sky like a half-moon heart. A killer concert band.

**Big Jack Reynolds, 1980s**
Toledo, Ohio

My great friend Big Jack Reynolds was earning a living as a plasterer when we met. He'd earlier recorded "Little Dog" for Fortune. We wound up playing together the last twenty years of his life. Jack never called anyone by his right name. I was always Rockford—crazy that way. Jack was around when my dad passed away and he kinda filled that void. A funny guy, he talked about how he "usta" sing to his mules and told this story about after he got drafted. I asked, "Jack, wha'cha do in the Army?" "Talked mostly, talked to the boys, gettin' them not to miss home. I was just real good to them, but I lost that job to Joe Louis, the World Champ." Never knew if it was true. That was Jack.

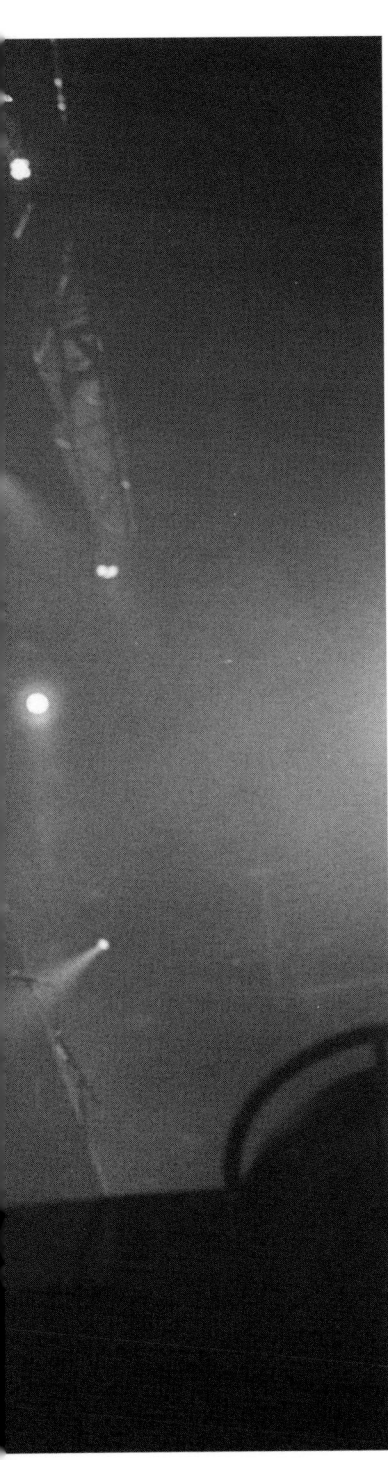

**Mick Jagger, 1980s**
Pontiac Silverdome
Detroit, Michigan

Mick at the Silverdome, struttin'. I'd taken pictures of the Stones when they opened the Voodoo Lounge Tour in East Lansing at the MSU stadium. You were allowed to shoot during the first three songs, then had to get away from the stage, so I took the film, stuck it in my jacket, tied my jacket around my waist, and headed back to a seat where my wife and friends were. Got there and the film was gone, I lost it. This shot's from my second go a few weeks later.

**Luther Allison, 1980s**
King Biscuit Festival
West Helena, Arkansas

Luther Allison, killin' the guitar. He was on Delmark Records and used to play around here a lot, but then moved to Europe because he wasn't makin' it in the United States. Then he came back and just tore it up. But, within a year, he had cancer and passed away. When he got done playing, it looked like someone dumped a bucket of water on him.

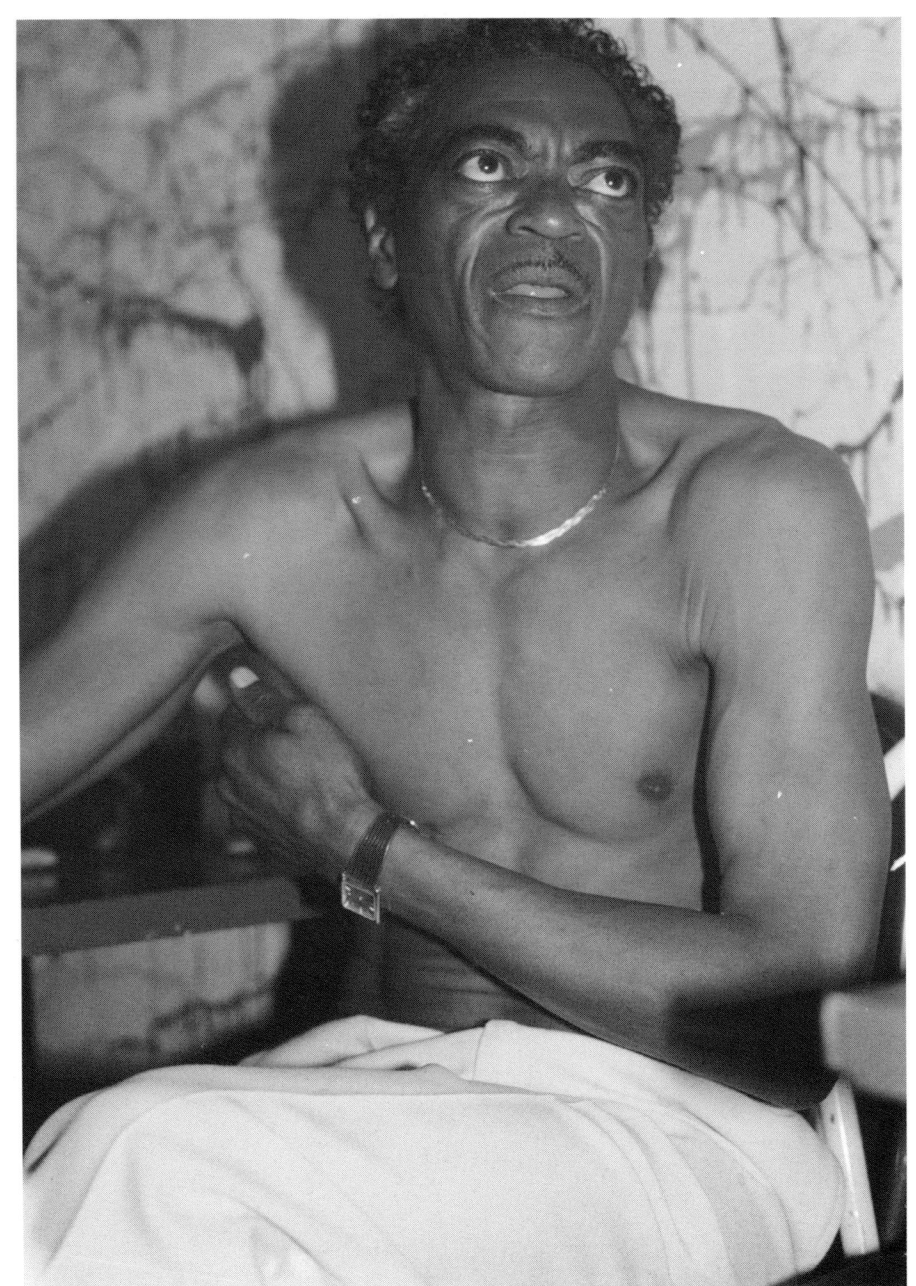

**Booba Barnes, 1980s**
Rick's American Cafe
Ann Arbor, Michigan

Booba Barnes was a blues singer with a hard rocking Chicago sound. He recorded for Rooster in the '90s and owned the Playboy Club in Greenville, Mississippi. This is backstage at Rick's American Cafe in Ann Arbor … an electric wild man, he's passed away.

**Riverside Motel, 1980**
Clarksdale, Mississippi

The Riverside Motel in Clarksdale used to be the G.T. Thomas Afro-American Hospital. In 1937, Bessie Smith died there after an automobile accident. Everyone from Sonny Boy to Ike Turner to John Kennedy, Jr. stayed in that place.

**Eddie Kirkland, 1980s**
Rock Rhythm & Blues Festival
Toledo, Ohio

The Detroit legend. He jumped off the stage during his version of "The Hawg." The guy was like in his 80s. Once, in Florida, he made a U-turn and hit a Greyhound bus. There used to be a White Tower downtown and that was like his station for business. So when he'd get into Toledo he'd call me and I'd be summoned to go, get him, meet him, and talk about recording and stuff.

**Terry Adams of NRBQ, 1980s**
Rock, Rhythm & Blues Festival
Toledo, Ohio

New Rhythm and Blues Quartet's Terry Adams, on the Maumee riverfront at Promenade Park. For about ten years in the '80s and '90s, Toledo-area beer distributors promoted the "Rally by the River" on Fridays, all summer and fall. You could count on a cold beer, great music, and huge end-of-the-week crowds. Man, downtown was hopping.

**Ruth Brown, 1980s**
Memphis, Tennessee

Ruth Brown, the Queen of R&B, at the annual Memphis W.C. Handy Awards. Struttin' her stuff, she claimed the stage.

**Solomon Burke, 1980s**

Chicago Blues Festival, Grant Park
Chicago, Illinois

A sanctified preacher with a great many children, he wore an outlandish suit that made him look like a general as he belted out "Everybody Needs Somebody to Love … and I need you, you, you! And I need you, you, you."

**Little Eddie King, 1980s**
B.B. King's Club
Memphis, Tennessee

The blues is so big. I mean it's a four-letter word up here and down South it's still what's up. Little Eddie was a killer blues performer.

**Bo Diddley, 1980s**
Chicago Blues Festival, Grant Park
Chicago, Illinois

One of rock 'n' roll's founding fathers, the great Bo Diddley, shortening the neck of his trademark square axe with a capo, singing "Hey Mona." Always sporting those big black glasses.

I got to open twice for Bo—once playing with the Homewreckers and once with Voodoo Libido. We were sent a set list and spent a couple weeks becoming Bo Diddley perfectionists, getting all the keys down tight. So, he comes to Toledo and I introduce myself and give him the set list of songs. Bo's in the bus driver's seat eating a baloney sandwich and he says, "You don't need that list. If I go like this, you stop. And if I go like this, you play. I'll see you on stage."

**Bud Spires and Jack Owens, 1980s**

Chicago Blues Festival, Grant Park
Chicago, Illinois

Jack played guitar and sang. His buddy, Bud Spires, usually accompanied him on harp. Betonia, Mississippi, is where they're from. They were doing Jack's tune, "Betonia, Mississippi Blues." Spires was blind and he and Jack were like the last of that Delta movement. The country blues thing is really pretty much gone now, but groups like The Carolina Chocolate Drops are trying to bring it back.

**Jerry Lee Lewis, 1980s**
Promenade Park
Toledo, Ohio

We played before him on the riverfront and did like two hours. I saw Roman Griswold out in the crowd and pulled him up on stage because we'd run out of material. All of a sudden this big black limo pulls up behind the bandstand. Jerry Lee jumps out and has two, three blondes with him. And he starts "You Win Again," by Hank Williams and I looked at my friend Dave Yonke of *The Blade* and said, "Forget about the Sex Pistols, forget the Clash, all these bad boys of rock 'n' roll." He's so talented, the baddest man on Earth, the killer—Jerry Lee Lewis.

**Robert Junior Lockwood, 1980s**
Ann Arbor Blues Festival
Ann Arbor, Michigan

Robert Junior Lockwood, Robert Johnson's stepson, sharing a laugh. Famous for the King Biscuit Show in West Helena, Arkansas, he moved up to Cleveland and lived there for years. Robert Johnson dated his mother and taught him to play the guitar and supposedly they'd be in Clarksdale and Helena and Robert Jr. would pretend he's Robert Johnson and Robert Johnson would do the other side of the river because, you know, two is better than one.

**Bobby Rush, 1980s**
Mary Manse College Auditorium
Toledo, Ohio

We're driving down Collingwood Avenue, back when Mary Manse College was still partially open, and I spotted a handwritten sign pinned to a phone pole—"Bobby Rush Tonite!" A couple blocks and we're there, man, in the old auditorium. Bobby Rush is a great harp player and does one funny, sexy show. You know, you just gotta keep your eyes open in the dark.

**Jake the Shake, 1980s**
Ann Arbor Blues Festival
Ann Arbor, Michigan

Nailed to the bone, looking good, and feeling fine, Ann Arbor street musician Jake the Shake wore the most outrageous clothes—plastic flowers, beads, and silk scarves. He carried a guitar, but I don't know if he could play it. Jake made up his own blues as he went along, all the while talking to voices only he could hear. People loved him. Jake represents a side of the music you won't see at the House of Blues.

**Muddy Waters, 1980s**
Ingman Room
University of Toledo
Toledo, Ohio

Muddy Waters in performance. A Buddha, he'd be in a room and everything would just shift. If he was just playing cards everyone still buzzed around him.

**The Reverend Al Green, 1980s**
Ann Arbor Blues Festival,
Ann Arbor, Michigan

Reverend Al pushing his guitar man to the limit and sanctifying his songs. Minister of his own church in Memphis, he turns songs like "Take Me To The River" into sanctified gospel. If you're ever in Memphis on a Sunday morning, there's only one place to be and that's in Al Green's congregation.

**John Entwistle, 1980s**
Promenade Park
Toledo, Ohio

The Who's John Entwistle was doing a solo tour and I was excited to meet him. I met him in the hotel lobby and picked him up, driving him over to the gig. Entwistle did like every Who CD cover and when a fan came over and asked, "Would you sign these?" he signed them all. Entwistle died in 2002.

**Sun Records, 1980s**
Memphis, Tennessee

Outside the Sun Records Studio, home of the blues, looking up at the classic yellow neon logo. Nothing retro, nothing fancy, but authentic and the best.

**Lynn White, 1980s**
King Biscuit Festival
West Helena, Arkansas

Real popular on the Chitlin' Circuit, Lynn White brought rhinestone dazzle to this annual October festival celebrating West Helena's deep blues heritage.

**Roman Griswold, 1980s**
Rock, Rhythm & Blues Festival
Toledo, Ohio

I swear Roman's fingers were twelve inches long. His hands looked like they'd been melted by the keyboard. My friend and occasional bandmate, playing boogie-woogie at one of the festivals in Promenade Park along the river.

**Paul Desmond, Dave Brubeck Trio, 1980s**
Masonic Auditorium
Toledo, Ohio

Desmond comes out looking like a high school math teacher and proceeds to cross all boundaries, playing his signature sax riffs and pulling up threads of deep traditional jazz. Brubeck's son's band, "Heavenly Blue," opened the show.

**Albert King, 1980s**
Masonic Auditorium
Toledo, Ohio

Albert King, on stage at the Masonic. I had a photo pass and went down to the dressing room while quiet Albert was smoking his pipe. A lovely man.

**Janis Ian, 1980s**
Masonic Auditorium
Toledo, Ohio

I interviewed her before the performance, then shot this picture of Society's Child Janis Ian after the show.

**Buddy Guy, 1980s**
Chicago Blues Festival
Chicago, Illinois

With fans and family along the River, Chicago's own Buddy Guy's been a Festival headliner almost every year.

**Tiny Tim, 1980s**
Ottawa Tavern
Toledo, Ohio

Everyone was Mister or Master or Miss to Tiny Tim. A huge guy, Tim wore funny suits and Depends, and did a bunch of sold-out shows at the original Ottawa Tavern on Bancroft Street, backed up by Steve Athanas' solid band "The Best." What a great club … till it burned down in the '90s. We threw a BBQ for him but he wouldn't eat anything, and after the party he went back to his hotel and had six whole Domino's pizzas. A true original.

**Detroit Junior and Little Smokey Smothers, 1980s**
Chicago, Illinois

Old friends Detroit Junior and Little Smokey Smothers talking and being easy backstage in Chicago.

**Lee "Shot" Williams, 1980s**
Chicago Blues Festival
Chicago, Illinois

I dig the sunshine coming through the little holes in the hat of Lee "Shot" Williams, a great soul singer.

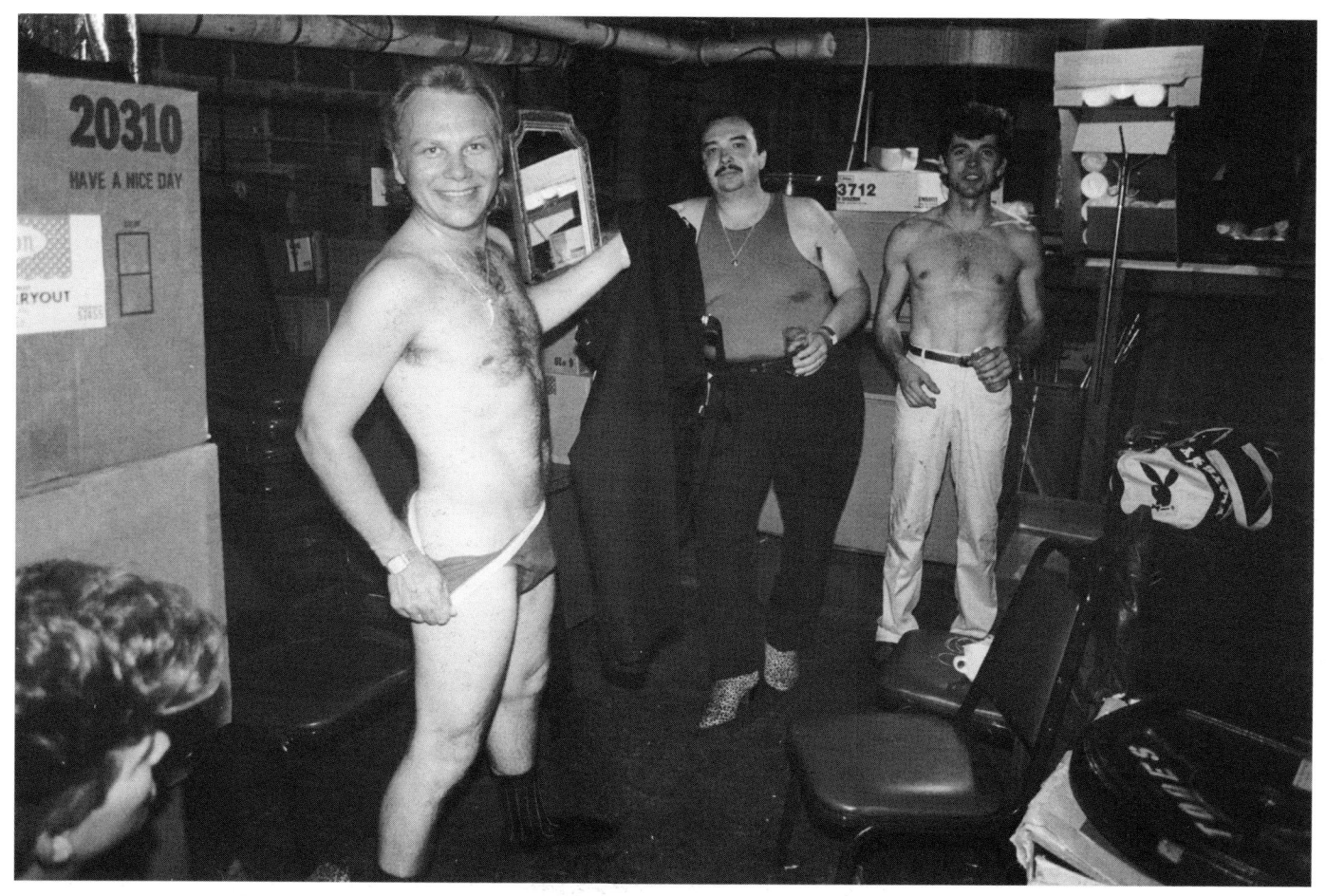

**Randy McDonald, C.C. Miller, Walter Salwitz, and Tony**
**The Dynatones, 1980s**
Ottawa Tavern
Toledo, Ohio

Break time for the Dynatones, just airing out between sets in the basement of the Ottawa Tavern. A dynamic, bone crushing, soul band led by Salwitz, Toledo's own Big Walter Shufflesworth.

**Eddie Harsh, James Cotton, and Kenny Neal, 1980s**
Ann Arbor Blues Festival
Ann Arbor, Michigan

Harsch was keyboard player for the James Cotton Band in the '80s and the Black Crows in the '90s, and Kenny Neal played in his dad's band as a kid and was Buddy Guy's bass player at eighteen.

**Otha Turner, leader and father of The Como Fife and Drum Corporation, 1980s**
Chicago Blues Festival
Chicago, Illinois

This guy farmed off Yellow Dog Road in Tate County, Mississippi, raising goats and chickens and crops, and had these famous wild-ass BBQ parties. Never got to one so I just know what I've heard. Turner recorded his first CD at the age of ninety and passed in 2003 at ninety-five.

**Eddie Kirkland's guitars, 1980s**
Toledo Blues Festival
Toledo, Ohio

Eddie Kirkland's guitar ammo on the hood of his ride! Eddie played Hines Farm when the club was renovated and reopened in 2003.

**Marcia Ball, 1980s**
Ann Arbor Blues Festival
Ann Arbor, Michigan

New Orleans style boogie-woogie piano queen, a fantastic soul singer, and one sweet stand-up lady with a devoted following that's almost cult-like.

**Bruce Springsteen, 1984**
Joe Louis Arena
Detroit, Michigan

You know how he is, getting the whole audience to sing ... Bruce's butt shot totally rocking the Joe.

**Dave Brubeck, 1985**
Masonic Hall
Toledo, Ohio

Total classic show featuring his son's band and his trio from the original "Time Out" sessions, Paul Desmond and Joe Morello. So it was a father-son show and people were still figuring out where this stuff came from. Brubeck was hip.

**Bruce Springsteen, 1985**
Pontiac Silverdome
Pontiac, Michigan

The young Boss, buff and beautiful, during the Born in the USA Tour. The E-Street Band performed marathon three-or four-hour shows, and Bruce's energy only got stronger and stronger.

**Dickie Betts Band, mid-1980s**
Main Event
Toledo, Ohio

This was a warm up tour for his band and there were only like 200 people at the show. Betts kind of snuck into Toledo unannouced without the usual pre-concert promo. This shot caught him downtown. He was incredible.

**Fortune Records and Big Jack Reynolds, mid-1980s**
Detroit, Michigan

Beginning in the '50s, Fortune Records, a small independent on Third Street in Detroit, recorded a lot of local guys in a little studio behind the record store, including Big Jack Reynolds and the Griswolds from Toledo.

Jack had recorded his first record there … "I had a little dog, his name was Bo …." And a bunch of little African-American girls show up, dancing around, playing hula hoop, and one asks Jack, "Are you B.B. King?" He takes his guitar, swings it around and says "…now, ain't that the shits?" Getting to Fortune was wild, with Jack shoutin', "Turn left here, turn there, there over by that burned-out house." The building's gone but the music's still around.

**Art Griswold, mid-1980s**
Toledo, Ohio

Easter Sunday, outside the old Theo's Taverna on Summit Street. I slipped out of Easter dinner for about a half an hour to run downtown. You can see everyone is having a ball.

**Eddie Shaw, Howlin' Wolf and the Wolfgang, mid-1980s**
Promenade Park
Toledo, Ohio

Eddie Shaw, saxophone player and bandleader of Howlin' Wolf's band, the Wolfgang. Shaw was back in Toledo in 2012, performing at the Rock, Rhythm & Blues Festival.

**Eddie "Guitar" Burns, mid-1980s**
Toledo, Ohio

Eddie "Guitar" Burns, a legend in Detroit, worked on lots of John Lee Hooker's records. While he took a break from a Blue Suit recording session, I took photos for the CD package.

**David "Honeyboy" Edwards, 1988**
West Helena, Arkansas

The incredible story Honeyboy tells is being in the Greenwood roadhouse the night of Robert Johnson's last performance and seeing Johnson so sick he crawled around on the floor and howled like a dog. He died the next day and Honeyboy helped bury him in a field. A couple weeks later when there was money enough for a proper burial, Honeyboy's family helped dig up the body and carry it away. Honeyboy recorded "West Helena Blues" on White Windows in 1989 for Blue Suit Records. He passed in 2011 after getting a Grammy for lifetime achievement.

**Stevie Ray Vaughan, 1989**
Toledo Zoo Amphitheater
Toledo, Ohio

I had met him in 1986 at the Sports Arena. Well, actually I didn't meet him. I had gone down to the Sports Arena to take pictures of him and was taking some shots and these guys were yelling, "Don't take any pictures!" So, I said I'd go to the other side and shoot. But the dude yells, "I said no pictures." I went over to my friend and said, "Let's get the hell out of here. This is awful." We hit the john and I'm taking a pee, and, man, all of a sudden these guys grab me and say, "Give me that film." Now, I knew where they were staying, so the next morning I went down and dropped off a picture of Son House and John Lee Hooker to let them know not everyone is a freaking idiot, that some of us are trying to preserve history or whatever, and document it. A week later I get a letter from Vaughan's manager saying next time we're in Toledo you've got total access. So I went to the amphitheater at the Toledo Zoo and took my wife, and Stevie was there and met us, took me around and said, "This guy is from *Living Blues,* he can do whatever he wants." Stevie Ray was totally energized, sober, and rocking, and I shot all night.

**Brian Setzer, The Stray Cats, 1989**
Toledo Zoo Ampitheater
Toledo, Ohio

Fried, dried, hair laid up to the side, Setzer and the
Stray Cats opened at the zoo for Stevie Ray.

**Lee Rocker,
The Stray Cats, 1989**
Toledo Zoo Ampitheater
Toledo, Ohio

Rockabilly personified, the Cats were high school buddies. Rocker's one of the great slappy upright bassists in rock 'n' roll and the amphitheater's a terrific outdoor venue.

**Ten Years After, 1980s**
Dressing room, Sports Arena
Toledo, Ohio

Ten Years After, kickin' back post-performance. Just another gig, a smoke, a drink, and a pretty girlfriend.

**The Griswolds, Toledo's Blues Brothers, late 1980s**
Toledo, Ohio

Art (left) and Roman Griswold, kings of Toledo Blues. They were unbelievable, would just play all night long. I remember putting a show together with them and Jack and our old band, The Haircuts, down at Wesley's on Adams Street. I was playing harmonica. There was a line around the block to get in. I started playing and it was like, "… well, I'll do a couple songs." Forty-five minutes later I'm dying and Art and Roman are going, "Hey, let's do another one." I took this picture 'cause they were going to Europe and needed some promo stuff. Roman died in 2012.

**Bob Dylan, 1989**
Savage Hall
University of Toledo
Toledo, Ohio

At UT, with his big band featuring Steve Douglas, who played sax and added that unique hook to all of Phil Spector's big hits. Dylan always surrounds himself with a stellar cast of great musicians and just keeps turning his songs inside out. Photographers could just shoot away all night at that UT concert. I've probably seen Dylan twelve to fifteen times in as many different incarnations.

# 1990s

**Cary Bell, 1990s**
Rock, Rhythm & Blues Festival
Toledo, Ohio

It was a cold afternoon with the wind blowing up the river and before he went on, Cary cups his mouth and asks me if I had any hard liquor handy. "No," I said, and he walked up on stage and just started wailing.

**Maria Muldaur, 1990s**
Rock, Rhythm & Blues Festival
Toledo, Ohio

When she was fifteen, Maria d'Amato was this pigtailed Brill Building prowler in a doo-wop chick group, "The Cashmeres." Then in the '60s, Maria married guitarist Geoff Muldaur and was a defining member of Jim Kweskin's Jug Band. She tells a great story about how Victoria Spivey took her under her wing, introduced her to classic female blues and the red-hot mama persona, and primed her career.

**The Motor City Soul Pioneers, 1990s**
Toledo, Ohio

We were doing a recording session in Toledo for Blue Suit with the Motor City Soul Pioneers. This is Kenny Clark (right) and Joe Frazier, and Kenny's wife, a spiritual person who would tell your fortune and read cards. During a break, we're listening to playbacks. The record came out pretty good.

**The Del McCoury Band, 1990s**
The Ark
Ann Arbor, Michigan

Bluegrass legend Del McCoury and his family band playing Ann Arbor's famously intimate Ark music club. Man, you know, it took a while for me to realize that a lot of bands are family acts.

**Duke Robillard, 1990s**
Unidentified venue
Toledo, Ohio

I caught Robillard with his trio at a long-shuttered club in downtown Toledo. The shots are murky and dark, but catch Duke's cool profile. He led Room Full of Blues for years and "The 1st Album" is horn-backed, gravelly New Orleans barrelhouse.

**Leon Russell, 1990s**
Westgate Pizzafest
Toledo, Ohio

Mr. Leon Russell, rocking the piano keys at the old Westgate Shopping Center, now gone. With a beer tent, pizza tent, and a one-night bandshell, the Westgate Shopping Center parking lot was packed and jumping. Leon's a chill dude.

**Charles Brown, 1990s**
Ann Arbor Blues Festival
Ann Arbor, Michigan

Charles Brown holding roses delivered to him from his friend Bonnie Raitt on his birthday.

**Ron "Crawdaddy" Crawford, 1990s**
Packo's at the Park
Toledo, Ohio

Crawdaddy, a gone Toledo legend and bad man with beautiful clothes! Nailed to the bone. A Voodoo Libido regular.

**Brewer Philips, Hound Dog Taylor's second guitar, 1990s**
Toledo Blues Festival
Toledo, Ohio

Brewer Philips was with Hound Dog Taylor's band and had just arrived in Toledo when I took this photo.

**Johnny Shines' guitar case, 1990s**
Chicago Blues Festival
Chicago, Illinois

A lot of blues miles on this case.

**Gaye Adegbalola, Sapphire The Uppity Blues Women, 1990s**
Toledo Blues Festival
Toledo, Ohio

Saffire's lead nasty … check out the crowd in her sunglasses. Political, tough feminist blues like "Bitch With a Bad Attitude" and "Too Much Butt for One Pair of Jeans" were their shout out, crowd busting favorites.

**Clarence "Gatemouth" Brown, 1990s**
Rock, Rhythm & Blues Festival
Toledo, Ohio

I first heard him play his funked-out Hank Williams sort of fiddle in New Orleans in 1976, with Professor Longhair on piano and a drummer surrounded by tribal congas. Gatemouth died after Hurricane Katrina. His house was flooded.

**Papa John Creech, Jefferson Starship, 1990s**
Anderson Arena
Bowling Green, Ohio

At this Jefferson Starship concert, Papa John played with Airplane survivors Marty Balin, Paul Kantner, and Grace Slick. One of the first blues fiddlers to play in a big time rock 'n' roll band, a dude who could frenzy up with a psychedelic outfit like the Starship.

**Lil' Ed & the Blues Imperials, 1992**
Labor Day Festival
Toledo, Ohio

You don't see the pipe on his finger here, but Lil' Ed played bottleneck slide guitar and was a wild man, totally drenched in sweat after performing.

**James Cotton, 1992**
Ann Arbor Blues Festival
Ann Arbor, Michigan

Harmonica master James Cotton, showing some wear before gigging in Ann Arbor.

**Sir Mack Rice, early 1990s**
Toledo Blues Festival
Toledo, Ohio

Sir Mack Rice is living in Detroit. He was an original member of The Falcons with Eddie Floyd and Wilson Pickett, and they had a song, "I Found a Love," that was a big hit. The Falcons broke up and Mack kept writing soul classics like "Cheaper to Keep Her" and "Mustang Sally," which is right now being played somewhere on this round, round earth. Mack sang "Sally" at both of my sons' weddings. He's blessed my life. I love the guy.

**Junior Wells, 1993**
Chicago Blues Festival
Chicago, Illinois

The great harmonica player from Chicago making a point. Very opinionated guy and snappy dresser, sportin' a brim, nailed, as they say, like a dog's dick.

**Lazy Lester and Steve Ferguson of NRBQ, 1994**
Big Jack Reynolds Memorial Concert
Toledo, Ohio

Lazy Lester was famous for saying "I ain't lazy. I'm just tired." Here he's with Steve Ferguson of the New Rhythm and Blues Quartet. They came into town to do a benefit for Big Jack Reynolds after Big Jack died. We did it at Murphy's Place downtown.

**Stephen Stills, 1995**
Rally by the River
Toledo, Ohio

Stills performed with Crosby, Stills, Nash & Young and solo, including this stop in Toledo. Just a gorgeous guitarist … after the end of his performance I asked him to autograph an album and he asked my name. I gave him my radio show handle, "Johnny Porkchop Dupree," and he said, "You're kidding," and I said, "No, that's it." The signed record's on my wall.

**Buckwheat Zydeco, 1996**
Columbus, Ohio

Buckwheat Zydeco [nee Stanley Dural] picked up his gilded accordian and burned down the house with his buddy on the scratch board.

**Harmonica Shah, 1997**
Juneteenth Festival
Toledo, Ohio

My friend, Detroit bluesman Harmonica Shah, at the Juneteenth Festival. They were booked for a UT concert and got me to get together a band. Shah drove his buddy's big green Detroit cab down to Toledo and right up to the front steps of the Student Union. Not bad service.

**Shardé Thomas, 1998**
Rock & Roll Hall of Fame Robert Johnson Tribute
Cleveland, Ohio

Otha Turner's granddaughter Shardé, playing the bamboo flute he made for her, at the Robert Johnson Tribute, "Hellhound on my Trail," sponsored by the Rock and Roll Hall of Fame. Shardé Thomas fronts her own fife and drum band now.

**Mick Taylor, 1998**
Cleveland, Ohio

Taylor, along with Bob Weir, Jimmy Vaughan, Peter Green, and other musicians, performed at Wilbert's, a Flats District bar, at the close of the celebration of Robert Johnson's music and life. Little did I know that a few years later in Chicago, I'd meet my guitar hero, Mick Taylor of the Rolling Stones, and introduce him to Eddie Kirkland, who'd just recorded a record for Blue Suit. Mick was a perfect gentleman and had great respect for Kirkland.

**John Mayall, 1990s**
Rock, Rhythm & Blues Festival
Toledo, Ohio

Father of the British Blues, he discovered Eric Clapton, Peter Green, and Mick Taylor. He finally winds up in Toledo.

**Elvin Bishop, 1990s**
Rock, Rhythm & Blues Festival
Toledo, Ohio

Elvin walks the crowd in Promenade Park with his wireless big red Gibson guitar. I once heard him say, "I don't know whether I want to be B.B. King or Merle Haggard, but I want to be somebody."

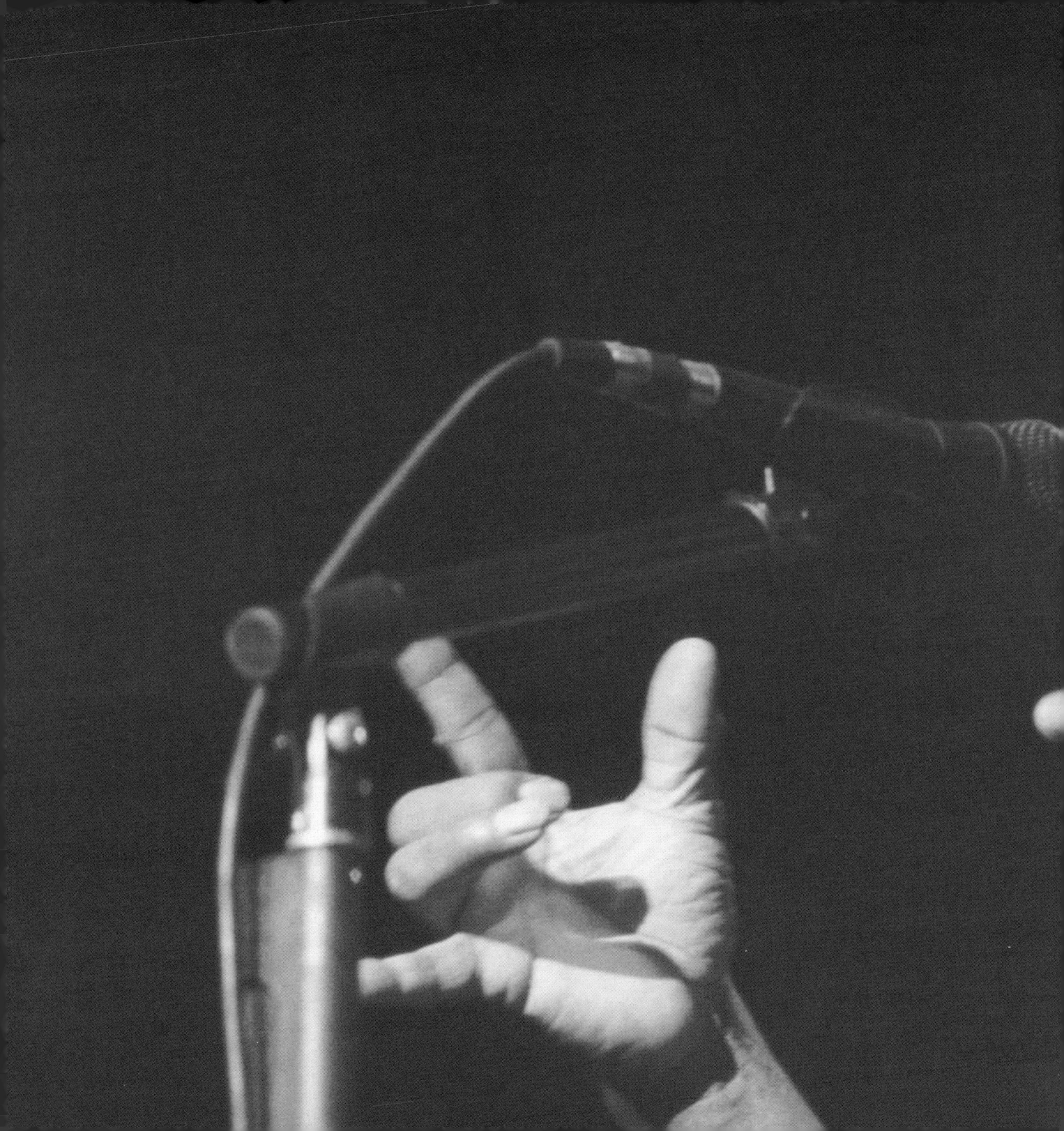

# 2000s

**Henry Butler, 2000s**
Art Tatum Jazz Festival
International Park
Toledo, Ohio

Celebrating Toledo's own Art Tatum on the east bank of the Maumee River, New Orleans' Butler was the headliner at the festival.

**Jon Hendricks, early 2000s**
Doermann Theatre
University of Toledo
Toledo, Ohio

The great vocalist rehearsing in Doermann Theatre at the University of Toledo. Jon came back to Toledo to live around 2000 and joined the university, celebrated his eightieth birthday at UT, and seriously is still teaching vocal jazz and performing at age 93.

**Buddy Guy, September 7, 2001**
DTE (Pine Knob) Music Theater
Clarkston, Michigan

This was the first big tour for my friend Tommy Castro, who played with the Dynatones. Buddy Guy came out. I took a front seat and got a great shot. He's an electrifying guitarist who moves from squeaky single notes to huge Hendricks-like high-pitched, soul-sacrificed, heart-blasting chords.

**Alberta Adams, 2003**
Toledo Blues Festival
Toledo, Ohio

Queen of Detroit blues, Alberta Adams kept getting better as she got older. She recorded for Chess Records in the 1950s and Cannonball in the 1990s. Love the rhinestone sunglasses.

## About John Gibbs Rockwood

Born in Cleveland, Ohio, John Gibbs Rockwood has lived in Toledo since his youth. He's a bandleader, blues singer, and harmonica player who performs under the stage name of Johnny "Porkchop" DuPre, fronting the band, Voodoo Libido. A blues impresario and co-owner of Grammy-nominated Blue Suit Records, his documentary photographs of musicians have been internationally published, exhibited, collected, and respected. Married to Jennifer and father of their adult sons, Ian and Julian, John is now the proud grandfather of Everett Rockwood, born February, 2013. *Can I Get a Witness* marks the first major collection drawn from the 26,000 plus Rockwood photos taken over the last forty years.

## Acknowledgments and Credits

"Cultural & Musical Treasures" [exhibition], Common Space & Toledo Jazz Society
"Muddy Waters: Can't Be Satisfied," [PBS, 2006]
"Singin' the Blues," *Footsteps* [Cobblestone Publications]
"The Best of Lake Erie West," in *Toledo* [periodical]
Backstage Gallery, www.backstagegallery.com/photographer/JohnRockwood.html
Big Boss Man: The Life & Music of Bluesman Jimmy Reed BK no date
*Big City Blues,* Periodical
*Blues Access* [#44, Winter 2001]
*Blues and Soul Records* #41 [Japan, periodical]
*Blues and Soul Records* #62 [Japan, periodical]
Bobo Jenkins Presents Big Star All Stars [Peavine Records Japanese label]
*Can't Be Satisfied: The Life & Times of Muddy Waters,* Robert Gordon [Little, Brown, 2002]
Chess Rhythm & Roll 4: 1960-1967 CD 1994
*Clarksdale Clarion*
David Honeyboy Edwards, Roamin' and Ramblin' CD 2008
David Honeyboy Edwards, White Windows [Bonus Tracks] CD 1988
David Honeyboy Edwards, White Windows CD 1988
Detroit Junior, Live at the Toledo Museum of Art CD 2004
Do What You Want Be What You Are: The Music Of Daryl Hall & John Oates CD no date
Eddie "Guitar" Burns, Detroit CD 1989
Eddie "Guitar" Burns, Second Degree Burns CD 2005
Eddie Kirkland, Democrat Blues CD 2004
*Exit Magazine* [Cleveland, periodical]
*For You—The Bruce Springsteen Book* BK
Frank Frost: Midnight Prowler [Earwig] CD 2003
Harmonica Shah, Motor City Mojo CD 2000
Hastings Street Band, Down on Hastings Street CD 1999
Howlin' Wolf, Ain't Gonna Be Your Dog CD 1994
Howlin' Wolf, Definitive Collection CD 2007
Howlin' Wolf, His Best CD 1997
*I'll Take You There: An Oral & Photographic History of Hines Farm Club,* Matthew Donahue [Jive Bomb Press] 1999
*Incurable Blues: The Troubles and Triumph of Blues Legend Hubert Sumlin* BK no date
Joe Weaver, Motor City Rhythm & Blues Pioneers CD 2002
John Lee Hooker, More Real Folk Blues: The Missing Album CD 1991
Katie Webster, Delux Edition CD 1991
Life of Bobo Jenkins [Peavine Records]
*Living Blues* [periodical]

Louis Collins, If Trouble Was Money CD 1996
Madhouse Gallery, [2010] exhibit
Martin Scorsese Presents The Blues DVD no date
Maurice John Vaughn, Dangerous Road CD 2001
*Mississippi Memories Volume 11: 1940-1999* [Clarksdale Clarion Ledger]
*Muddy Waters: The Mojo Man* BK no date
*Popular Music and Society* V3 #2 [1974], Bowling Green State University
Robert Lockwood, Jr., Steady Rollin' Man CD 1970
*Rolling Stone Magazine*
*Rolling With The Stones,* Bill Wyman  BK no date
Roosevelt Sykes,  Ann Arbor Blues & Jazz Festival, Vol. 3 CD 1996
Sir Mack Rice, Right Now CD 1992
Sun Ra, It Is Forbidden CD 2001
*Swamp Watch* [Black Swamp Blues Society, periodical]
*The Toledo Blade*
*The Blues Story*
The Griswolds, Cockeyed World CD 2001
*The Light in Darkness* BK
*Toledo City Paper*
Various Artists, Chess Blues CD 1992
Various Artists, Chess Rhythm & Roll CD 1994
Various Artists, Hastings Street Grease: Detroit Blues Is Alive, Vol.2 CD 1999
Various Artists, Straight Outta Burbank: The Bomp! 25th Anniversary Collection CD 1999
VH1, "Legends: BB King," September, 1997, MTV Networks
Victoria Spivey, Grind It CD 1999
*Waylon: A Biography* BK
WBGU-TV, "Hines Farm," documentary film no date
*Witness to the Blues* [Toledo Poets Center Press, 1999]
www.artistdirect.com [artists' credits]

# Index

3D, 60, 68
Ace, Johnny, 22, 25
Adams, Alberta, 157
Adams, Terry, 76
Adegbalola, Gaye, 134
Allman, Gregg, 10
Allison, Luther, 72
Anderson, Ian, 49
Atlanta Rhythm Section, 47
Bad Company, 12
Baez, Joan, 46
Ball, Marcia, 103
Barns, Booba, 73
Bell, Cary, 124
Betts, Dickie, 108
Bishop, Elvin, 149
Blakemore, Ritchie, 13
Brooklyn Blues Busters, 25
Brown, Charles, 130
Brown, Clarence "Gatemouth," 135
Brown, James, 32
Brown, Ruth, 77
Brubeck, Dave, 106
Bowie, David, 33
Burke, Solomon, 78
Burns, Eddie "Guitar," 112
Butler, Henry, 152
Clark, Kenny, 126
Cornick, Glenn, 14
Crawford, Ron "Crawdaddy," 131
Creech, Papa John, 136
Cotton, James, 106, 138
Desmond, Paul, 92
Detroit Junior, 97
Diddley, Bo, 80
Dixon, Willie, 19
Dural, Stanley, 143
Dylan, Bob, 121

Dynatones, 99
Eagles, 53
Edwards, David "Honeyboy," 113
Entwistle, John, 88
Ferguson, Steve, 141
Frampton, Peter, 34
Frazier, Joe, 126
Frey, Glenn, 53
Green, The Reverend Al, 87
Griswold, Art, 110, 119
Griswold, Roman, 91, 119
Griswolds, 119
Guy, Buddy, 95, 150-151, 155
Hall, Daryl, 36
Hammond, Ronnie, 47
Harsh, Eddie, 100
Havens, Ritchie, 44
Hendricks, Jon, 153
Hooker, John Lee, 22, 31
House, Son, 28
Howlin' Wolf, 26
Hutto, JB, 38
Ian, Janis, 94
Jagger, Mick, 41, 71
Jake the Shake, 85
Jenkins, Bobo, 31
Jennings, Waylon, 8
Jethro Tull, 49
J. Geils Band, 68
Kantner, Paul, 61
King, Albert, 93
King, B.B., 48
King, Freddie, 23
King, Little Eddie, 79
Kirkland, Eddie, 75
KISS, 6-7, 59, 67
Lazy Lester, 141
Leadon, Bernie, 53